THE NIXON POEMS

THE NIXON POEMS

BY EVE MERRIAM

ILLUSTRATED BY JOHN GERBINO

ATHENEUM   1970   NEW YORK

To

the Constitution of the United States of America

THE NIXON POEMS

POST-INAUGURAL | I cannot pronounce his Presidential name.

Still stumble over it
like getting up at night
and groping down the hall
where is the bathroom door?
eyes closed all the while
swaying holding on to the wall
then padding back to bed
pulling the pillow over my head.

As though descending into personal shame.

SPRING | The sky
is as blue
as policemen's helmets.

PROGRAM | When the new President
introduced his cabinet

he sponsored them
on evening primetime

presenting them as men who all have
"that extra dimension"

and if the Presidential phrase
seemed fuzzily familiar or shopworn

from being bandied about
for brands of cigarettes   cough drops   shaving cream containers

well what's wrong with
a bona fide business connection?

SHADE

★96
★97
★98

SHADE

★68
★99
★95 ★69
★66
★94 ★67
★70
★100
★65

73 74
★71 75 76
72 ★ ★ ★ ★ SHADE
87 ★ ★63
88 SHADE 62
89 85 ★ 86 64
83 80 60 ★101
84 56 57 52
82 81 79 61 59 55 53 51
90 77 58 54 102
93 92 78 50
38 37
32 91
39 33 36
31 34 35
14 1
30 29 11 2
28 10 7 6 3
40 27 13 SHADE 9 SHADE 4
12 8 5
41 15
42 26 17 18 19
16 22 21 20
23 START 49
25
43
24 48
47
46
44 45

6

DICKETYDICKETYDICK

dicketydicketydick
dicketydicketydick
click

priorities goals directions
     smile solemnly see direction A
click

great country endeavor great leadership
     inspirational fist follow fig. 2
click

forefathers return to forward new day dawn
     arms up and out see direction AB foldover dotted line
click

responsibilities meet quality of life contribute
click click

wind back
kcidytekcidytekcid   kcidytekcidytekcid

VIEW

A new building
has gone up
with
no spaces for windows.

if we can send a man to the moon we ought to
clean up the what do they black want
power students should be fire with fight now you
take if they just would law and listen but they
scared to walk down the black even in the day
power something's got to why doesn't the mayor do
noise every time you turn on the confront
easy get it anywhere just like a sixpack
or carton of let it all go up in black
garbage the garbage where are you going to stack
the planes on the highways crawling with all
black but they won't it is power there's no place to call
your breathe in the prices higher and higher every soon
if we can send a man to the moon

NETWORK

Did the eyes go first?   punched in like eggs
next arms and legs neatly clipped   more economical for
Packing   then torso baled   the liquid blood siphoned off not a
teardrop spilt   one must marvel at how silently the majority
shape was fashioned

PROPOSAL FROM AN OFFICE BUILDING

Spring is delightful.
How pleasant now to sit out
on a park bench and munch
daffodils
instead of a dry egg sandwich at the desk.

April, I'm loving you!
Make six copies
and keep the original
in the top file drawer.

THINGS | It is after midnight
and the things in the stores long to be taken out

their feelings are too much for them
the rows of plastic made to look like leather
the ranks of leather smooth as any plastic

they long to be taken out of themselves
to be distracted
so they will not weep here in the dying dark

they long to become men women and children
sitting smiling watching the television war.

WORKING HIS WAY THROUGH

None of the magazine subs he is offering door-to-door
have dirty pictures
or suggestive language
only clean wholesome family funsportsleisureslaxand
workshop hobbies
with current events and civics next to
the crossword puzzle and budget recipes

and he is so sincere when he makes his pitch
you just know he is going to become
top salesman
and keep on plugging and rising
until he could become head of the whole company
and even President of the United States someday
if only he weren't already

SAFEGUARD

is the name of
the anti-ballistic missile system
which
—if all works well—
will defend us
again and again and again
from nuclear death

and

SAFEGUARD

is also the name of
a deodorant soap
widely advertised
and piled in the stock of
your local supermarket

although
most doctors state
that washing with plain soap and water
is enough to kill germs
and the anti-bacterial agents added
are not only unneeded
but could irritate the skin of sensitive people
and even in some cause cancer

lather
therefore
with care

FOUND IN AN ESTABLISHMENT FORTUNE COOKIE

If you
puke upon me
I shall
cover
it
with velvet and sequins
and sell
it
back
to you.

NOWADAYS | I wake in the morning
with a stone in my head

a stone in my heart

stones for legs

and I
walk.

FASHION NOTE IN WARTIME | high as
as this
are week's
skirts body
the count

1. **Pre   Fix**

He declared a National Day of Participation
for stepping on the moon

                              "pause
                              to
                              mark
                              the
                              moment
                              of
                              transcendent
                              drama"
                              the teleprompter unreels

He declared the holiday in advance
suppose they don't land

well, we could always keep it as
a National Day of Mourning

          There is a nixon style
          everything is good for something

2.

"Since the Creation"

Already the race to litter is on
smearing the moon
with the American flag wired to wave "forever"
and the plastic plaque encasing the Nixon name

> below
> born for the times
> the prayerful Billy Sunday faces of astronaut parents
> mother quavery-voiced father gruff
> What are the Russians doing with a satellite up there
> I thought we had the prime space all blocked out

and the commercials still orbiting their round
as history takes place on the tv screen
the moment caught as Armstrong speaks to the camera
"one small step for a man   one giant leap for mankind"
canned cant from and for the p.r. boys
nevertheless

> thrill
> the fell of black beyond the atmosphere
> the dazzlement of craters struck by solar light

and the first human setting foot
Adam up there joined by his fellow
jumping and clumping in their sci-fi suits

> in and out of shadow
> waving like a slow motion dream

the lunarscape is real
seen and reseen the scene
something to grab onto
to get away for a space
from our daily nightmares
our madeup mad concocted stories
of war on earth
                of failure of nerve
                        of death by rivers of waste

3.

Lan   Ding

Here comes the blessed sanctimoonious moral
Machine can but try
Man (Americ) does better

as the craft
programmed to set down
on the Sea of Tranquility
might have crashed to doom
had not at the controls
Neil Armstrong
(mister armstrong civilian, see how you mere citizen
control the dickystate?
the military is but your good strong Arms)

snatched from the lunar railroad track
from the lunar mortgage foreclosing
on all those space company stocks and bonds
NASA fallen to new funereal lows
but up in the nick of
lucking out
Armstrong!
(boyish all-amer-i-can-do)
in command

charged on

and manually landed
in the clear

so build thou more stateside computers o my soul
as God goes   so   up   man

4.

Divine   Calling

He prezzes the button and
telephones the moon

Hi Neil   Hi Buzz   Prez Here
this must be the most historic phone call ever made huh
heh
howzit up there heh
heh taking some good pictures for us
well good that's great boys it's great really
talking to   you take it easy now

Hi Thieu   Hi Ky   I'm getting us out
all out   right away
never should have been there to begin with

Hi Reps   Hi Sens
we don't need any more overkill
let's cut the mirvs and double medicare

but he stays with the moon

PENTAGONIA

Perhaps sharks act that way
because we mistrust them.
Why don't we try loving them
for their sharkly lovable qualities?

For their shark teeth,
for their snapping jaws,
for their gulpability.

CO.

A smell
rides up on the escalator with me

as we ascend

higher and higher the stench
from the factory
stamping medals for the Nixon era
of shit cast in bronze.

ABM ABM

If someone attacks me I must be prepared.
That is why I keep a fierce watchdog by the door
and train him to bark at first sight of the foe.

I have bought flash cards for the dog,
manuals, and maps of the enemy's possible route.

The dog eats a great deal of high protein meat,
and although he is blind and deaf, has a cold healthy nose
and his coat is glossy and strong, patches rarely fall out.

THE PRESIDENT AS KING OF THE GODS

1: Of Jovial Laughter

He places in the throne room
souvenir matchboxes that read
"Stolen from the Jupiters."

2: And Junoesque Proportions

After the ambrosia
she dabs at her dry lips
and folds the clean paper napkin
to use again.

TO BE CONTINUING

No
Never
Not
I will not be the first American president
to lose a war
I will not preside over defeat

if I am to be swallowed up by history
let the whale be in my belly

the dead in Viet Nam
           bloat
           mount
                  s   p   r   e   a   d

UPPER WEST SIDE STORIES

1.

What do I do about this beggar in the subway car?
His homemade cardboard sign
is hung by string around his neck:
"My mother has
multipal Scleorosis and I
can't See out of my Left Eye. Please
help Us thank You."
Dark pants, dark shirt, dark as
the sweat on his darker face,
he holds out his hand the unblind phoney
lurching past me the fake the phoney
can see better than I can
as
good officer in the war on poverty
I drop fifteen cents of hatred into his hand
and the insolent black bastard
doesn't even salute.

UPPER WEST SIDE STORIES

2.

We should get together more often says 4C
yes and not wait for emergencies says 3B
yes says 5A it used to be we had meetings
against raising the rent says 2D
and not having garbage collected often enough says 3F
against cockroaches says 5E and the leaky pipes
but now it's so crowded says 4G
and everybody's so busy says 5B
all we get together for says 2C
is after the murder in the self-service elevator.

UPPER WEST SIDE STORIES

3.

If God had wanted the Spanish here
He'd have made them English-speaking
the white-bobbed old lady
with white chin whiskers
and white anklets like Easter lilies
sprouting from
her black bulbous shoes

having voted out the Civilian Review Board
and prematurely celebrating Mother's Day
with a pink paper carnation
that opens wide to spell
Put Prayers Back Into Public Schools

rises on shining wings
to scream at the anti-war pickets
and dreams of dying her saint's death
miraculously
ridding the neighborhood once and for all
mercifully
of all those niggerkikes.

UPPER WEST SIDE STORIES
4.

The German super limps and drinks.
Soft and unprussian,
he is cheerful about putting in a new light bulb for the hall;
cheerful but forgetful.
The hall stays dark.
Good morning, his boozy cheer calls out,
as he wrestles with garbage cans and gunnysacks of paper,
kicks an abandoned sofa in its floral upholstered rear.
The stuff some people throw out, he snorts.
Quickly looks up,
I don't mean some people special,
I get along with all kinds,
all kinds we have here, that's what makes it America,
I mean the stuff that people any people throw away,
like this sofa
why even some white people would be happy to have it.

Ah well, he kicks it along,
I'm going to fix that hall light
tomorrow for sure.

CHECKLIST

Action
Authentic
Companionship
Ethical
Family
Fidelity
Fresh
Genuine
Honest
Ideal
Individual
Joy
Life
Living
Pride
Purpose
Trust
World

CHECKLIST

ACTION: Used principally to describe carbonated beverages, toothpaste, aspirin. For specific usage, see "the bubbling-action soda," "the foaming-action toothpaste," "the quick-action headache reliever."

AUTHENTIC: A reproduction, as in "an authentic reproduction of early American."

COMPANIONSHIP: Quality denoting the relationship between an animate object and an inanimate one, such as "the companionship of an outdoor motor," power tool, pop-up toaster, electric blanket.

ETHICAL: Drug requiring a prescription.

FAMILY: A series of cars or food products, such as The Family of General Motors or The Family of General Mills.

FIDELITY: (a) see **TRUST**; (b) hyphenated with **HI-**

FRESH: Associated with **FACTORY** or **FROZEN**; cf. "factory-fresh cigars," "frozen-fresh orange juice."

GENUINE: See **AUTHENTIC**.

HONEST: An unmentholated cigarette.

INDIVIDUAL: A single portion.

LIVING: Suffix of **BETTER**, surrounded by a kitchen.

PURPOSE: Compound with **ALL**, as in "all-purpose cleaner."

TRUST: A bank.

WORLD: Of pleasure, of satisfaction, as in chewing gum.

IDEAL, JOY, LIFE, PRIDE: These are all copyright brand names and the use or pursuit thereof is restricted to the properly identified product, viz.: Ideal is a dog food, Joy is a detergent, with Life there is a choice of three—magazine, cereal, or filter-tip cigarette—and Pride is a floor wax.

PINKVILLE

and atrocities
don't happen all that often
and only a few took part
and are nothing compared to what the other side does
and after all have always been part of war.
and we deplore war
and always have
and always will

ANDand&@
  AND
  A N D

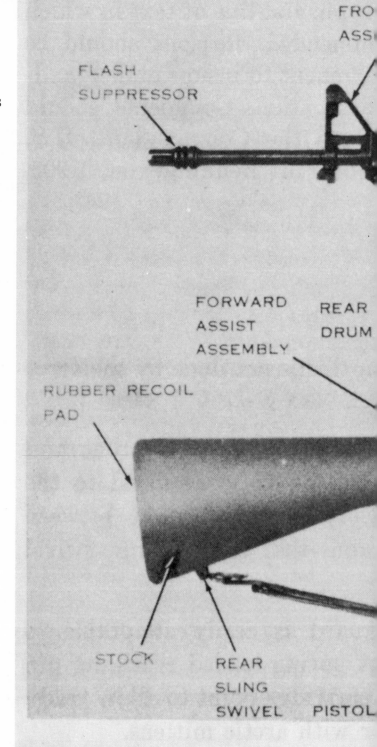

FLASH
SUPPRESSOR

FRO
ASS

FORWARD
ASSIST
ASSEMBLY

REAR
DRUM

RUBBER RECOIL
PAD

STOCK

REAR
SLING
SWIVEL

PISTOL

Figur

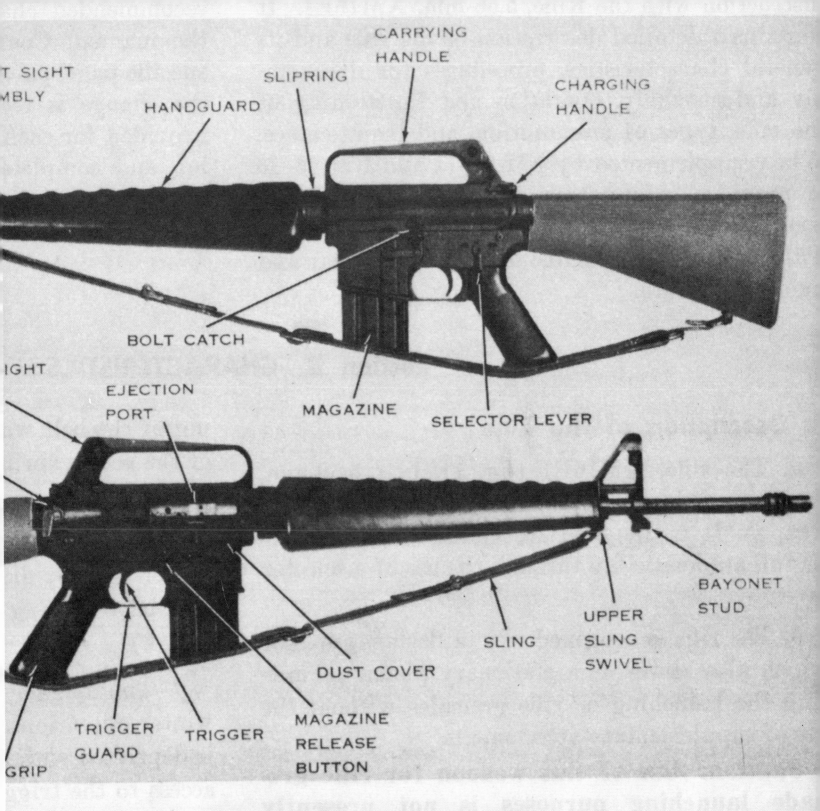

Figure 1. Rifle, 5.56-mm, XM16E1, right and left side views.

STATESMANSHIP

Let me fake one thing perfectly clear
We and the Government of South Viet Nam
have announced we are prepared to accept
any political outcome which is arrived at
through free elections

MY PREZ

of whom
else can I say
that
when he does
something good
there is
a bad reason for it

MY NIXON DREAMS

1.

I am in the White House
smiling
feeling guilty
hug and squeeze him and
say Peace
guilty but for a good cause
he squeezes back
friendly not sexy
Peace
I know he doesn't mean it
but I stay

MY NIXON DREAMS

2.

He is driving the car
his foot on the brake
brake doesn't hold

he tells us it's dangerous
we should get out

Who are we all?
I can't see
but I get off
drop from the car

he drives on
the brake works
and there's no danger
he's bluffing

then I'm in a big room
reading a headline
World   Contagion   Plague
it is serious
but he still wasn't telling the truth

44

TRYST

When we were married eight years,
we saved up enough money
for my husband to buy me
an engagement ring.
I wear it to the office
to take dictation from the boss,
but then when I go to type
I take it off and
hide it in my cosmetic bag,
you never know with the
messengers or temporaries
the agencies send around.
Then when I finish up
at the end of the day,
I go to the ladies' room and
hang it on a chain around my neck,
that way I don't have to
worry in the subway.
Cooking or doing the dishes,
I hide it in the candy jar
mixed in with the mints,
nobody would ever look there
and sometimes I find new places
like in the plaid stamp books,
it's hard even for me
to know all the nooks where I put it.
Sometimes I think
when I take off my nightgown
for us to make love
I ought to put it on,
it's really beautiful,
but there's enough
to worry about then on my mind,
I don't want
more responsibility.

QUIZ

How did the great cities fall?

Was there a snowstorm
and uncollected garbage
in Thebes?

Did the ceremony to the altarplace
have to be protected
by bulletproof chariots
and spears on the
Cretan rooftops?

Who will be left for the taking of tests
that offer multiple choice answers
to the end of our ☐ age
                                    ☐ nation
                                    ☐ world
                                         ?

HUBERT HORATIO HUMPHREY

"Water appears to be my natural habitat,"
the fish allowed,
"but perhaps that is only because
I have not yet experienced dry land
or a frying pan."

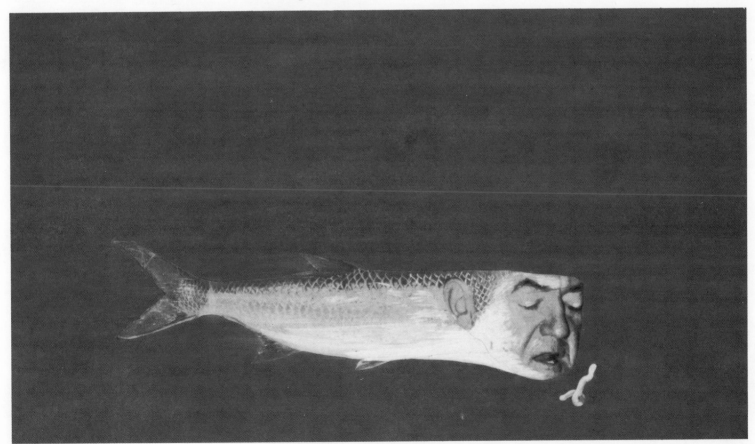

CINDERELLA: TAKE ONE

Swept and shoveled and scraped and scrimped
and saved
only a dollar a week
but that was enough to
purchase a winning lottery ticket
entitling her
to 1 fairy godmother
1 pumpkin coach drawn by mice footmen
good for 1 passage to ball and return by midnight of same day
only

and after the ball was over
and the prince disappeared
and she needed an abortion

at the rate of saving only a dollar a week
she had the baby
and was lucky enough
to be given
her old job back
and who knows
the baby might grow up to
purchase a winning lottery ticket of its own

CINDERELLA: TAKE TWO

In the grand ballroom

posed for pictures as
Princess of Poverty

and was congratulated by celebrities
who deprecated themselves murmuring
It's you everybody wants to meet
and How much more Charming she is than Anyone giving a
Damn suspected

and she would receive all the proceeds

just as soon as
the committee took care of
the expenses of running the volunteer office
and paying the salary of the professional publicity director
and full page ads in the New York Times announcing
contributions were tax-deductible.

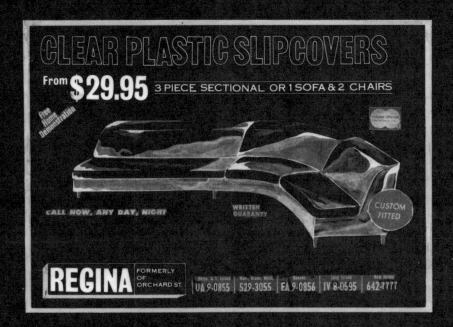

THE PEACEABLE KINGDOM

Sunlight streaming into the suburban window
where the housewife was cleaning curtain rods
and the two-year-old whined for his diaper to be changed

busy cleaning the rods
kept on whining
hit him with the rods and he fell onto a toy truck

knocked unconscious but
didn't die until four hours later

where the eight-month-old baby slept in the crib
soundly through all
and the three-year-old watched As The World Turns
during the sunbright afternoon

TROOP CUTBACK

We now have
in the field
fewer
than last month

and

far fewer
than
next month

SPIRO PROPOSES

A toast:
To Mars
by the end of the century!

And to getting out of Viet Nam by
what is that embarrassment
that static in the sound
that blurring image
that something that keeps on hanging there in the picture
wavering like a thread?

AGNEW LADY

in the bank
blanches before
two tall blacks
one with a sombrero
black shirt
black bellbottoms
the other
dotted and striped and
tall as a basketball player

Is it a stickup?

she draws back as
they deposit a check
and cash one
and go out
quietly

she knows they are
a front
but
for what?

LETTER TO THE EDITOR

Dear Sir: whatever happened to
the sweet butterchurn mornings
and the tow-headed boy on his bike
flipping onto the porch
the afternoon paper
with its news   faraway
of trouble spots   faraway
in the distant night   faraway   ?

THE DRAW

During his administration
the draft became a lottery

young men reaching age 19
learned what their chances were
of reaching 20

drawing high low or jack in the middle
seemed as sensible a way as any of figuring
out

        haphazard
        as killing of or by the enemy

or
for accidents
happen
being knocked off by ones own goodguy side
unwitting
unremitting

COMMUNITY COUNCIL: NARCOTICS

Every citizen should be aware of the symptoms of the narcotic addict. This information has been compiled in order to assist you in combatting one of the city's largest problems.

Recognizing the Addict

   a. Needle marks, scabs, on arms, legs, etc.
   b. Pupils of eyes dilated when in need of drugs.
   c. Excessive nasal secretions.
   d. Nodding, drowsiness and unconsciousness.
   e. Possession of drugs or equipment.
   f. Self-isolation regularly 4 or 5 hours apart.
   g. Dry mouth, nose or itching of same and licking lips.
   h. Chain smoking.
   i. Increased consumption of sweets, i.e., candy, soda.

Recognizing the Drugs

a. Heroin—White or slightly brownish powder, resembling powdered sugar. Nearly always found in glassine envelopes.

b. Marijuana—Resembles ground, dried-up weeds and grass. It is a mixture of dark green and light brown particles and seeds. Usually found in small brown envelopes.

c. Glue—Airplane glue normally used. Placed in brown bag, inhaled with face inside bag. Glue generally on face and clothing. Youth usually smells strongly of glue.

d. Pills—Found in various forms and shapes. Many resemble cold capsules, tablets, also injected in liquid form.

Hiding Places

a. Various body cavities.
b. Taped to body, i.e., bandage.
c. Under washbasin, sink, tub.
d. Medicine cabinet in odd containers.
e. Under carpets.
f. Rear and bottom of drawers.
g. In refrigerator.
h. Inside closets, coats, suitcases.
i. Rolled up in windowshades.
j. Rooftops of tenements.
k. Apartment house landings.
l. Areas adjacent to schools.

The finding of any of the above should be reported to the Precinct.

LANDSCAPING

Some of
the more expensive lobbies
now have
mixed in with the artificial
so cunningly
you can scarcely tell they are
real plantings

only when
brown spots appear
can you be sure
they are real
because then you know they are
dying

VEEP | The clown puts on his lightbulb nose
his floppy shoes   his pompoms and polka dots
flaps around in the ring
squats in the crudest spots
watch honey he's going to do something real funny

falls down on a horn that honks his behind
veep veep   hoo ha aooGAH
Mister Dumb Bunny   Mister No Mind

and falls in the sawdust and falls again the stupe
the poopypoop   veepa veepa

smacked in the kisser his nose lights up veep
like a red cherry smash sockimagain flash flash

now clap while he takes a bow
wipes off the white chalk   the black eyes
removes the putty nose and comes up with
a truncheon
and waves it

look isn't he a scream with that rubber salami ha ha
and climbs the stands beating up everybody who laughed

hey this is good it's part of the show it's only fool
what is this clown doing make him step down
somebody do something get this clown to stop call a cop
somebody call the authorities get through to the highest
my god Mister President it's up to you you're the only one
who can stop this
CLO
  w
      w
          w

TEXT FOR A MEDIA MASS

(Coffin. Flowers. Candles. Organ.
Mourners get up to podium,
speak, then return to seats.)

Speaker One:
(Mother)

When I was first married,
I made my own spaghetti sauce.
But now with the children and all,
I haven't time.
One day I discovered
Ronzoni—
it was the same kind of sauce
I'd been making myself,
with no starch
or artificial fillers.
It was terrific.

Speaker Two:
(Father)

What I said was
Show me just one filter that won't
take away the taste and
I'll eat my hat.
New Lucky Strike Filters
put back the taste others
take away.
You get—unchanged—
Lucky Strike's famous fine-tobacco blend.
And Lucky's Flavor Tip
actually enhances the taste.

Speaker Three:
(Brother)

Once you choose the right car,
the dealer who uses the GMAC plan
can help you fit it into the family budget.
He'll arrange everything
right in his office.
Help you save needless expense—
remember, the cheapest way to buy on time
is to pay down as much as you
comfortably can,
then pay the balance
as soon as you can.

Speaker Four:
(Sister)

The stainless steel head
has lasting sharpness.
And it's washable, too.
The head snaps off
to rinse clean.
And you get the fastest motor.
Impact-resistant case.
Anywhere.
Anytime.

Unison:

Kingsize. Queen. Super. Economy.
Crackle. Smooth. Satiny. Pop.
In the name of the One Ninety-Eight,
the Two Ninety-Eight
and the Three For Five Dollars.

LITTER

We used to use it for landfill
like a seven-layer cake of dirt,
garbage, dirt, garbage, dirt,
garbage and then the icing of
good top dirt.
Now there's almost no place left to fill in.
Only a few marshy spots
and the conservationists are raising hell:
leave the swamps alone,
the wet, the mosquitoes, the squawking birds,
leave a little hunk of malarial nature.
So where do we stash?
It's still cheaper for the paper manufacturers
to grow more trees
than try compressed ways to use the old stuff.
Hitler was a neat stacker.
Maybe, in reverse,
we could find human beings valuable once again,
more so than the Christmas wrapping, than the coffee table book,
people becoming a new status symbol in themselves:
look, I'm more disposable, easier to bend me, break me,
rend me into dust sans residue.

NIX   **ONIX**   **ONIXO**

If only we could
Nix   on
and then
Nix   off

N   O   X   O   N   I
    X   N   O
I   N   I   N   N   X

                X   O   N
                N   I   X
                O   I   N

                        x   n   x
                        o   x   o
                        i   x   n

                                            x   n   x
                                            i   x   i
                                            x   o   x

THE DEMOCRAT IN THE WOODPILE | I love the whole damned world.
Even the foreigners.

ROBIN HOOD | has returned
to Sherwood Forest
as
Secretary of the Interior

and the greenery
is to be preserved
for the public good

directly alongside
the parts reserved
for Hood Enterprises

for Sherwood Homesites
Shop-and-Sher Parking Plaza
and
Sherburger Franchises.

Having grown not horn   nor hoofs   nor giant insect antennae
but turning into him

I congratulate Edgar Hoover on his 130th birthday in office

I demand that the Southern school system definitely begin to
integrate except for weekdays holidays and Leap Year

I call upon Attorney-General Mitchell to seek new tasks now the
Panthers have been eliminated

I invite Billy Graham to bless the official White House
bowling alley

METAMORPHOSIS I lead the crusade against air pollution by ordering supersonic jets

I lead the crusade against noise pollution by declaring the
silent majority

I lead the crusade against water pollution by a secret plan that
will be revealed at the proper time

I exhort our darker brethren to get a piece of the action by setting
up black capitalism in the George Washington Carver peanuts
bank

I appoint a new Supreme Court Justice not to appease Strom
Thurmond but George Wallace

And anoint myself for bed beseeching good football-watching
weather

And I do not change

DARK AGES

there is no magic
that can force
the frog prince
to emerge
upright

he may stay
in the marshes
croaking his croak
until we
croak

KING RICHARD'S ARTHUR | and his Knights of the Round Table advise
and he makes Excalibur perfectly clear

EVERYDAY

The uniform
patting it in place

the undercover man
the bulge inside his shirt

the lawyer
strapping it in his briefcase

the doctor
under the stethoscope in his bag

the cabbie
inside the glove compartment

the window cleaner
along with the squeegee in his bucket

the storekeeper
in the cigar box behind the cash register

the secretary
in the bottom drawer of the filing cabinet

the bartender
back of the apricot brandy

the washroom attendant
in the broom closet next to the paper towels

the lady
poking the handle into her pearl evening purse

the teacher
sliding it into the folder among the test papers

and the pupil
learning
every day

an everyday way of life

O

"Your Majesty should not listen to the words of
other people, there is no pestilence in this country;
it is as healthy as ever. And my lord well knows that
I am not given to writing flatteries to my lord . . . the
perfect, the gorgeous, the offspring of heaven, our
protective angel, the expert and effective warrior,
the light among his brothers, the shining gem, the trust
of all important persons, endowed with nobility, the
provider for scholars, the table laden for all people,
outstanding among his peers, to whom the gods have granted
a treasure of grace and riches." —A MIDDLE BABYLONIAN, 1800 B.C.,
IN LETTERS FROM MESOPOTAMIA*

O

Osiris of the Overworld
Occupant of Highest
Office
O Commander-in-Chief
Of all Our Armed Forces
O
Olympian Appointer
Of Supreme Justice
O
Orchestrator
Of Anti-Communist Orgasm
O
Outstanding Opportunist
O
Orthopedist of Democratic Deformities
O
Optimum
Operator
O
Outright Nixon's the
One

*Translated by A. Leo Oppenheim (University of Chicago Press, 1967).

FLAGS

1. Let all the horns honk patriotism
   hoo hoo hooray
   hey

   buddy
   move over for Old Glory
   move outatheway (whatsamatter you a cripple or somepin)
   so what if theyre not making front parlors any more
   put it in the front parlor window
   be ProuD

2. its still a courageous country
   where even a Vice-President
   dare speak his heart and mind

   expanding on windshields
   supplanting dashboard madonnas and babyshoes
   affixed to urinals in filling stations

3. hurry up get the
   key i cant wait
   why dont they keep it open oh
   but then just anybody
   could walk in free
   and you cant have that no of course not its property
   a flagpole
   and fringed cord
   mating

4. on stamps   on shopping bags   on kiddiekarts
   set into cufflinks   rhinestone pins   haircurlers
   painted on the made in Japan handpainted tie
   dogflags wagging   watch dont step in
   catflags meowing
   here kitty liberty   here kitty liberty
   birdflags flying
   treeflags branching
   fishflags burbling

Old Glory waving

in the crotch of the hootchiekootchie topless

6. if youve got it   fly it

from ashtrays highball glasses matchcovers

paper napkins coasters wall plates decals calendars surfboards

sweatshirts watchbands head scarves pendants belts earrings curtains bathmats

it could go on like

Charlie Brown or The Beatles   a classic

7. on the conversation-piece

cigarette lighter shaped like a gun

flash it

on the plastic visors of helmets

on mooniforms

on gas canisters

on lilac time heritage old colonial deodorant sprays

on cockroaches with red white and blue shining carapaces

salute pray and eat

pizza with hot sausage stars

red pepper and mozzarella stripes

fingerlickin good glory hallelu

8. of thee

whee!

on the biggest slot machine in Vegas

programmed to come up every time

instead of cherries or berries or bells

ring it out dingdong killcong dingdong

God bless   God Bless   god Bless

GOD US

dont worry God   America is on your side

The Protest Marchers

        Little Red Riding Dick

The Protest Marchers

        loops through the woods

The Protest Marchers

        to visit

The Protest Marchers

        dear old Grandma Dick

The Protest Marchers

        who turns into

The Protest Marchers

        Big Bad Trick Dick

The Protest Marchers

        who quickly wolfs down

the protest marchers

        and turns back into

The Protest Marchers

        dear old Grandma Dick

The Protest Marchers

        and dear Little Riding

The Protest Marchers

        while

the protest marchers

        mass in the streets

The Protest Marchers

        and

the protest marchers

        disperse

the protest marchers

LETTER TO THE EDITOR: REVISED

Dear Sir: do you remember
those happy oldtime riots
when they burned
and stoned
and stayed
mainly in
the faraway
part of
town
    ?

OBSERVE THE FOLLOWING RULES OF SAFETY WHILE WALKING THE STREETS

1. Try not to walk alone at night—have someone accompany you through the streets.
2. Have a friend or relative meet you at subway station or bus stop.
3. When you arrive at home—ring your bell to alert a relative or neighbor. Have a key ready in your hand to open door.
4. Don't enter an elevator with a stranger of any age.
5. Walk in an area that is well lighted—don't take shortcuts.
6. Know the location of police call boxes and public telephone booths in your area.
7. If there are doormen in your neighborhood know when they are on duty they may be helpful.
8. Remain alert while walking. Look around you.
9. If you observe any person or group that appear suspicious do any of the following:
   a. Use a police call box and call for assistance.
   b. Go to a public phone booth and dial 911.
   c. If no phone is available enter any store or residence and then call the police. Persons in the neighborhood are willing to help.
10. Try not to carry large sums of money, conspicuous jewelry or other valuables; when you cannot avoid this, secrete the cash and other valuables on your person—not in your wallet or handbag.
11. Don't place your house key together with other keys, keep them separate. If you lose identification papers together with your house keys someone may have access to your home.
12. Carry a whistle or a cheap battery-operated alarm that emits a loud buzzing sound when a pin is extracted. These are sold in radio, 5–10 cent and department stores.
13. Carry your purse close to your chest. Don't dangle it loosely at arm's length.
14. If at any time of the day or night you hear screams or cries for help—pay attention—try to pinpoint their origin and location. By helping your neighbor you help each other. Dial 911.

**ACTION
TO TAKE
IF
YOU ARE
A
VICTIM**

1. Remain calm—try not to panic. Very few victims of a mugging or a purse snatch are injured, if they remain calm.
2. Don't resist or try to overcome a perpetrator.
3. Study the perpetrator if you can. Note his description—height, build, approximate age, facial features, articles of clothing, etc.
4. Call police as quickly as possible over police call box or public telephone 911—remain patient.
5. Notify the police in every case. Reports of every crime are necessary to help us assign patrolmen where needed.
6. Wait for the arrival of police—don't leave.
7. When arrests are made cooperate with the police and the courts.

The COMMUNITY and POLICE working TOGETHER will reduce this PROBLEM.

WHITE HOUSE SOUTH

The Orlon Banlon Nylon Nixon vacation home
in Key Biscayne is a few miles north of where
giant African snails have begun to infest the
neighborhood.

Imported by an eight-year-old boy who bought them
as a gift for his grandmother, at first count
three years ago there were only three of the large brownish
things.

They thrive on foliage and eat the paint from houses
to get calcium. Says the area administrator for the
Florida agriculture department, "Conventional poisons
don't bother them. One solution could be to eat
them."

There are thousands upon thousands of these giant snails now,
breeding.

AESOP IN WASHINGTON 1: The Fox and the Grapes

"The grapes are sour," said the fox when he couldn't reach
the vines. "I'm going away, and now you won't have me to stick
around anymore."
And went
and got boosted
and hoisted
and lifted up
and stood on top of
and hustled
and piled and piled
and finally plucked the grapes.
"What a wonderful country," he said,
"where a creature lowly as me
can grow."

MORAL: High office can accommodate to any level

AESOP IN WASHINGTON 2: The Lion's Share

The military lion, the workhorse, the long hare, and the peace dove went hunting for funds.

There was the question of how taxes should be divided. "Quarter them," roared the lion; so the other creatures divided the sum into four equal amounts.

Then the lion pronounced judgment:
"The first quarter is for me in my capacity as forward freedom fighter against communism;
the second quarter is for me as chief of defensive nuclear balance;
the third is for me because the cost of everything is going up;
and as for the fourth part, well just try and get it out of the arsenal."

MORAL: Your money and your life

AESOP IN WASHINGTON 3: The Swallow and the Other Birds

It happened that a farmer was sowing seeds in a field where a swallow and some other birds were hopping about picking up food.

"Beware of this farmer," said the swallow. "That is hemp seed he is sowing; be sure to pick up every one of the seeds or you will regret it."

"Nonsense," twitted the other birds, "the farmer is our friendly protector. Look at the birdbath and bird feeder he puts out for us."

Soon the hemp seeds grew into tall plants and the plants were made into cord and of the cord nets were made to catch the birds.

MORAL: Don't look to the Justice Department for justice

AESOP IN WASHINGTON 4. The Lion and the Mouse

Once when a lion was asleep a little mouse began running up and down his mane. This soon awakened the lion who placed his huge paw over him and opened his jaws to swallow him.

"O King of the Beasts," said the mouse, "I pray you to let me go! Who knows but that one day, small as I am and great as you are, I may yet be able to do you a favor."
The lion lifted up his paw and let him go, for the little creature was not worth thinking about.

Some time after, the lion was caught in a trap and bound round with strong ropes. The mouse came by and the lion said,
"Now, my little friend, you can help me. Gnaw at these ropes and let me out."

The mouse shook his head. "Nobody can get you out of this one. It's a Southeast Asian trap."

MORAL: Leave Viet Nam to the Vietnamese

AESOP IN WASHINGTON 5: The Boy Who Cried

There was once a young shepherd tending his flock all alone. "Help, help!" he cried out. "Smog is polluting the grazing land!"

But nobody listened.

A short time later he cried out, "Help! O please help! Nerve gas has killed the sheep by the thousands!"

Still nobody listened.

Then he called out, "O look, a black panther carrying a gun."

And everybody came running.

MORAL: Out of God's mouth into public relations

AESOP IN WASHINGTON 6: The Crow and the Pitcher

An elderly crow, nearly dead from thirst, came upon
a pitcher that had very little water in it
and he could not reach his beak far enough down to get at a
single drop.
Wearily he took a pebble and dropped it into the pitcher
where it made a slight splash. Then he dragged another
pebble across the ground and dropped that into the pitcher.
Then another. Then another and another.
At last the little bit of water was near the top and
he would finally be able to drink.

Just then a shot rang out and broke the pitcher and the water
trickled out to the ground.
"At least it didn't hit me," said the crow as he died of thirst.

MORAL: There has to be a generation gap

89

AESOP IN WASHINGTON 7: The Hare and the Tortoise

The hare was so swift that none of the other
animals could beat him. One day, however, the tortoise challenged him to a race.

The hare laughed. "You! Of all the slow creatures! Surely you aren't serious!"
"Yes, I am," said the lumbering tortoise. "Let us have a contest and see who will win."

So a track was agreed on, and the two set out.

Immediately the hare darted ahead, while the tortoise
crept by inches. The hare soon got bored and decided
to take a nap.
It was such a long nap that when he awakened, the tortoise was almost at the finish line,
but the hare sprinted and won easily.

"Why did you challenge me to a race?" asked the hare.
"Didn't you know I would win, no matter what?"

"Of course," said the tortoise, "but somebody's got
to make it look as if the two-party system works."

MORAL: Power to the powerful

OUT OF THE SMITHSONIAN | those posters from 1960:
Would you buy a used car from this man?
that darkjowled scowlbrowed smile smile you're on
smile

and in '68
furbished the posters anew
Would you buy a used war from this man?
while

we ponder for '72
Would you scar a planet with this used man

as we pile in the patched-up car
that commutes to the war on the moon

PHENOMONIX | where my President basks in the Southern sun,
a strange new era has begun.

Live catfish have started appearing on land.
Oozing out of the Florida swamps,
first the creatures flop onto sand;
then they actually walk on their fins,
as though each were a foot or a hand.

Standing upright, they travel for miles each day.
Wishing will not drive them away.

Stalking the highways at dawn;
at midnight are still walking on.

Loathsome unnatural sight:
can one accommodate to fright?

Where my President basks in the sun,
an era has begun.

HAIRY/SCARY | youth
grows
like tendrils   like curly pubic vines

growing
their sideburns and beards
dark as jews

growing
even when theyre sleeping
jesus

creeping
choking
clogging

growing
thicker and
crazywild

like pedestrians
outrunning cars
it cant be done

| BRING US TOGETHER

It's a free country said the man swinging an ax-handle at his
    neighbor
You can say that again said the neighbor swung against and
    swinging back
And the great thing about US said the woman swinging her
    handbag
Is everybody can express theirself said the woman smacked in
    the eye by the handbag and
Swinging back at the student carrying a placard for peace and
Being swung along by the shouts of
End the war   Burn the war down   Smash the windows of war